More STORIES And SONGS Of JESUS

Paule Freeburg, D.C.
Christopher Walker
Illustrated by
Jean Germano

OCP PUBLICATIONS

This Book Belongs To

More Stories And Songs Of Jesus
© 1999, OCP Publications
5536 NE Hassalo
Portland, OR 97213 U.S.A.

Music and text © 1999, Christopher Walker and Paule Freeburg, DC
The new translation of *The Lord's Prayer* from the English Language LiturgicalConsultation (ELLC).
Illustrations © 1999, Jean Germano
Published by OCP Publications
All rights reserved

CREDITS:

Publisher — *John J. Limb*
Editorial Director — *Paulette McCoy*
Executive Editor — *Joanne Osborn*
Project Editor — *Mary K. Straub*
Editing Assistance — *Scot Crandal, Geraldine Ethen, Kathy Orozco, Angela Westhoff-Johnson*
Music Engraving — *Sharon Norton, director; Laura C. Kantor, Christine Ambrose*
Graphic Assistance — *Patricia Burraston*
Art Director — *Jean Germano*

More Stories And Songs Of Jesus

Book .... edition 10417
Stereo Cassette *(Stories and Songs)* .... edition 10418
Stereo Cassette *(Songs only)* .... edition 10419
Compact Disc *(Stories and Songs)* .... edition 10420
Activity/Coloring Book .... edition 10421

Stories And Songs Of Jesus

Book .... edition 9404
Stereo Cassette *(Stories and Songs)* .... edition 9405
Stereo Cassette *(Songs only)* .... edition 10010
Compact Disc *(Stories and Songs)* .... edition 10610
Activity/Coloring Book .... edition 10019

Edition 10417
ISBN 0-915531-78-X

Printed in Mexico

Introduction

For Children

   More Stories And Songs Of Jesus has been written for you to hear and sing about the best friend in the world. Many of you got to know Jesus and some of the things he did in the first book, *Stories And Songs Of Jesus.* This new book has more stories about all the wonderful things Jesus did. There are lots of new songs for you to sing to help you remember what happened to Jesus and his friends and also to help you talk to Jesus. Remember, he is always your friend. He will listen to you and help you in good times and bad. So talk to him, and don't forget to listen to what Jesus wants to tell you!

For Parents

   This book, like the first volume, is for you to enjoy and share with your children. Read the stories out loud and sing along with the music. Bedtime is a good time for sharing a story and a song. The first volume has become popular on long car journeys and we hope this one will too!

For Teachers and Catechists

   Stories And Songs Of Jesus has proved to be a useful teaching tool from kindergarten up to second grade and even further. Like the first book, *More Stories And Songs Of Jesus* can be used as a basis for your Religious Ed. Program. By using it imaginatively, you can help children in their first experience of prayer. Later, children will experience this in greater depth when they start attending Children's Liturgy of the Word; but it is never too early to talk to Jesus as your friend.

   Read the stories out loud to the children or let them read to you. Children need to experience all varieties of music and not just one kind, so the songs have been written in all styles from 'pop' to classical and folk. Some of the songs retell the story, others take an idea from the story and relate it to the children's lives so that they will feel a real connection. When singing the songs in class, encourage the children to add extra sounds such as fingersnaps and clapping and actions, too. They can also play percussion and other instruments. Simple percussion can be added to the more rhythmic songs.

   Many of the rhythms are so infectious that children will find it difficult to keep still—don't stop them! The more children use their bodies in music-making, the more they are involved and can remember the songs!

   Your children will have fun putting on a musical. Choose a balanced selection of the stories, and perform them with children as narrators as well as actors for the characters. Your children's choir can sing the songs. Add variety by having solo voices doing the verses.

Yours in the love of Jesus,
Paule and Chris

Table of Contents

Table of Contents

Joseph Was A Good Man

1. Jo - seph was a good man, a good man, a good man,
2. Jo - seph heard an an - gel, an an - gel, an an - gel,
3. "Ma - ry's ba - by, Je - sus, Je - sus, Je - sus,

1. Jo - seph was a good man, cho - sen by the Lord. And
2. Jo - seph heard an an - gel cho - sen by the Lord. "The
3. Ma - ry's ba - by, Je - sus is cho - sen by the Lord. And

1. Jo - seph loved __ a la - dy, __ Jo - seph loved __ a la - dy, __
2. la - dy you __ will mar - ry, the la - dy you __ will mar - ry, the
3. he will save __ his peo - ple, __ he will save __ his peo - ple, __

1. Jo - seph loved __ a la - dy, __ cho - sen by the Lord.
2. la - dy you __ will mar - ry is cho - sen by the Lord.
3. he will save __ his peo - ple __ cho - sen by the Lord.

A long, long time ago there was a man called Joseph who lived in the town of Nazareth. Joseph was a carpenter. He made chairs and tables and lots of other things out of wood. Joseph loved a woman named Mary very much. And Mary loved Joseph too, because he was a good and honest man. They were going to get married. But then Joseph found out that Mary was going to have a baby. Joseph didn't understand that her baby would be born by the power of the Holy Spirit, and he didn't know what to do.

One night while he was sleeping, God sent an angel to talk to Joseph in a dream. The angel said, "Joseph, don't be afraid to get married. Mary's baby will be born by the power of the Holy Spirit and he will be called 'the Son of God.' You will name her baby Jesus and he will save his people."

When Joseph woke up, he did what the angel had told him to do. He went to Mary and said, "God spoke to me in a dream and told me not to be afraid. Let's get married now!"

And so they did.

9

To Egypt

Capo 3: **(C)** Eb   **(Fmaj7)** Abmaj7   **(C)** Eb

1. An an – gel spoke to Jo – seph in a dream.
2. "Take Ma – ry and her ba – by, quick – ly, go,
3. So Jo – seph took the ba – by, Ma – ry's child;
4. When all was safe, to Naz – a – reth they came.
5. And Je – sus grew in wis – dom, full of grace,

(C) Eb   **(F)** Ab

1. The an – gel said _____ to Jo – seph in a
2. and hur – ry down _____ to E – gypt, quick – ly,
3. in E – gypt he _____ pro – tect – ed Ma – ry's
4. The ho – ly fam – 'ly to Naz – a – reth they
5. so we could live _____ for ev – er full of

(G) Bb   1-4   5

1. dream: _____
2. go." _____
3. child. _____
4. came. _____
5. grace, _____

5. so we could

(Dm) Fm   **(Cmaj7/E)** Ebmaj7/G   **(F)** Ab   **(C)** Eb   **(Dm7/A)** Fm7/C   **(C)** Eb

5. live for ev – er full of grace. _____

Do you remember the story of how Jesus was born in Bethlehem? Mary and Joseph couldn't find anywhere to stay, so Jesus was born in a stable. Shepherds and wise men came to see him. Then the shepherds and the wise men went back to their homes and told everyone that they had seen Jesus, the Savior. Now this is what happened after Jesus was born in Bethlehem.

One night while Joseph was sleeping, an angel of the Lord talked to him again in a dream. The angel said to Joseph, "Hurry, get up. Take Mary and the baby Jesus and go as fast as you can to Egypt. The bad king, Herod, wants to kill Jesus. Stay there until I tell you that it is safe to come home." So Joseph got up at once and quickly got everything ready for the long journey. Joseph, Mary and the baby Jesus left for Egypt that very night. It was a long way from Bethlehem and the roads were hilly and rough. They were very tired, but at last they came to Egypt and found a place to live.

They stayed in Egypt a long time waiting for God to tell them it was safe to return home. Then one night while Joseph was sleeping, the angel came again and told him in a dream, "The bad king Herod is dead. It is safe for you to go home now." So Joseph took Jesus and Mary home to live in Nazareth.

I Belong To Jesus

1. I be-long _____ to Je-sus, _____ and I love him I
2. I will talk _____ to Je-sus, _____ 'cause I love him, I
3. I will stay _____ with Je-sus, _____ 'cause I love him, I
4. I will fol - low Je-sus, _____ 'cause I love him, I
5. I will walk _____ with Je-sus, _____ 'cause I love him, I

1. love him. I be - long _____ to Je - sus _____
2. love him. I will talk _____ to Je - sus _____
3. love him. I will stay _____ with Je - sus _____
4. love him. I will fol - low Je - sus _____
5. love him. I will walk _____ with Je - sus _____

1. _____ ev - 'ry day, _____ I be - long _____ to
2. _____ ev - 'ry day, _____ I will talk _____ to
3. _____ ev - 'ry day, _____ I will stay _____ with
4. _____ ev - 'ry day, _____ I will fol - low
5. _____ ev - 'ry day, _____ I will walk _____ with

1-5. Je - sus _ ev - 'ry day.

Once upon a time there was a man called John. He was Jesus' cousin. His mother was called Elizabeth and his father was Zechariah. John lived a long way out in the desert. He believed in God and wanted to do whatever God asked him to do.

One day God said to him, "John, I want you to tell the people that the Savior is coming. Help them get ready to meet him." So John told the people, "Try very hard to live the way the Savior wants you to live. Be kind to each other and help other people. If someone is poor, give them a coat. Never lie or cheat people. Always be honest and tell the truth." Then John took them into the Jordan River and baptized them.

One day while John was baptizing some people, Jesus came to the river. He went up to John and said, "Please baptize me, too." John said, "But you are the Savior. You should baptize me." Jesus said, "No, John. I want you to baptize me." So John baptized Jesus in the Jordan River.

When Jesus came up out of the water, he was praying. Then the people heard God say, "This is Jesus, my son, and I love him very much."

The Friends Of Jesus

1. Mat-thew, Ju-das, Phil-ip, Bar-thol-o-mew, An-drew, Thom-as, Si-mon,
2. Je-sus called the twelve __ a-pos-tles, and he calls us just the

1. Jude, James and John and James and Pe-ter the Rock. These are the a-
2. same. When we hear the voice of Je-sus the Lord, we will lis-ten

C/G G   C   Dm/C Cmaj7 F/C   G/C F/C Cmaj7 Dm/C | Last time
                                                     | C

1. pos-tles' names. ____
2. for our name. ____

14

Once there was a man called Matthew who lived in a town in Galilee. Matthew collected the taxes from the people in his town. But Matthew was a bad tax collector. He was not honest and he cheated people out of their money. People thought Matthew was a sinner and a bad man.

One day when Jesus was walking, he saw Matthew sitting in his office where he collected the taxes. Jesus called out to him, "Matthew, stop what you are doing, and follow me." Matthew looked up and saw Jesus, and right away he got up and followed him. Matthew was so happy that Jesus wanted to be his friend, and he said to him, "Jesus, will you come to my house for dinner?" Jesus said, "Yes, Matthew, I want to have dinner at your house." Matthew invited his other friends so they could meet Jesus, too.

When some of the people heard that Matthew invited Jesus to his house, they became angry and said to Jesus, "Why are you going to Matthew's house? Matthew is a bad man and you shouldn't be eating with him and those other sinners." Matthew felt very sad when he heard the people saying these things about him. But Jesus said to the people, "I want to be with Matthew and his friends. I came to help people who do bad things, but who want to change and do good things."

Then Jesus said, "People who are healthy don't need a doctor. People who are sick need a doctor. It's the same way with people who do bad things. They are the people who need me the most, and I came to help them do better. I came to help people just like my friend Matthew." And Matthew became one of Jesus' special friends; they are called the "apostles."

Talking To Me

Dm   C Dm   Dm   C Dm   Dm   C Dm

1. "Why are you talk – ing to
2. "What are you giv – ing to
3. "Come and see Je – sus, the

Bb   C

1. me, ask – ing me for a drink? ____ Just think what the
2. me? How can you give a drink? ____ Just think! For you
3. Lord, for the wa – ter he gives, ____ it lives! And by

Dm   Gm   C   Dm

1. oth – ers would say, __ if on – ly they could see
2. don't have a buck – et. Liv – ing wa-ter for free ____
3. this liv – ing wa – er, al – ways we will live

G9   A7   Dm   C Dm   C Dm

1. you're talk – ing to me." ____
2. you're giv – ing to me." ____
3. with Je – sus, the Lord. ____

D   C   D   C   D   F#m

rall.   *slower*

1-3. "I will give _ you liv – ing wa – ter,

G/B   D/A   G

1-3. so that you __ will live for ev – er, so that you __ will

Em/A   D   Am6/C

1-3. live for ev – er. I will give __ you liv – ing wa – ter,

16

1-3. so that you __ will live for ev – er, so that you ____

1-3. ____ will live for ev – er." 3. "For

3. ev – er, for ev – er."

One day Jesus was walking from Judea back to Galilee where he lived. It was a very long walk and the road was very dusty. On his way, he stopped at a town in Samaria. It was the middle of the day and it was very hot, so Jesus was tired and thirsty. He sat down by a well because he wanted to get a drink of water.

After a while, a Samaritan woman came with her bucket to get water out of the well. When Jesus saw her, he said, "Please give me a drink of water." The woman didn't know who Jesus was and she was surprised that he was speaking to her, because the people where Jesus lived didn't like the people from Samaria. So she said, "I am surprised you are talking to me. I am from Samaria and you are a stranger here. Why are you asking me for a drink?" Jesus said to her, "If you only knew who I am, you would ask me for water, and I would give you living water."

The woman didn't understand what Jesus meant, so she said, "You don't even have a bucket with you! Where will you get this living water you are talking about?" Jesus said, "When you drink the water from this well, you will always get thirsty again. But I am talking about a different kind of water. The water I will give you is living water, so you will live forever."

Jesus was telling her about being baptized in water and about living in heaven forever. The woman believed Jesus and went running off to tell all her friends about him. She said, "Come and see the man who told me, 'I will give you living water so you will live forever.'"

I Can See

1. Je-sus met a ___ blind man who could not see. His friends said, "Je-sus,
2. Je-sus said to the blind man who could not see, "I real – ly want to

1. touch him 'cause he wants to see." So Je – sus took him to a
2. help you to ___ trust in me." So Je – sus looked up-on the

1. qui – et place a – long the way. He made some spit ___
2. man and said, "Be – lieve in me," and touched the man a –

REFRAIN *(Faster)*

1. ___ and put it on his eyes ___ that ___ day. Je – sus asked him,
2. gain ___ so that he could clear – ly ___ see.

"Can you see, can you see, can you see?" Je – sus asked him,

"Can you see, can you see ___ me?" The blind man said, "Yes,

I can see, I can see." The blind man said, "Yes, I can see,

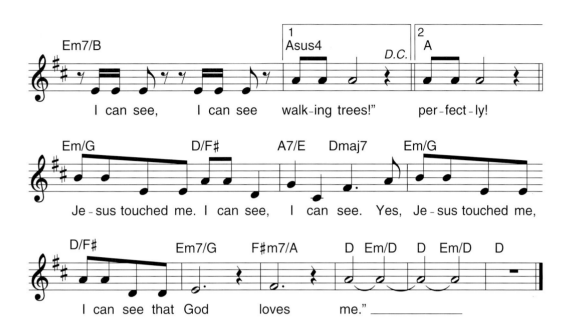

I can see, I can see walk-ing trees!" per-fect-ly!

Je-sus touched me. I can see, I can see. Yes, Je-sus touched me,

I can see that God loves me." _____

One day Jesus and his friends went to a town called Bethsaida. There was a man living there who was blind. Some of his friends took him to Jesus and they asked him, "Would you touch our friend? He is blind, but we know you can heal him. If you just touch him, he will be able to see." Jesus said, "Yes, of course I will help your friend." And he took the blind man by the hand and led him away from everyone so that they could be alone.

Jesus made spit and put it on the blind man's eyes. He put his hands on the man's head and prayed.

Then Jesus asked the man,
"Can you see anything?"
The man said, "Yes, I can see
something. I can see people, but
they look like trees walking around."
So Jesus touched the man's eyes again and
said, "What can you see now?" The man said,
"I can see you, I can see everything perfectly!"
Then Jesus and the man went back to their
friends. And everyone was happy because
the man could see.

Have Faith, Believe In Me

REFRAIN

Have faith, be - lieve in me. __ Have faith, be -
lieve in me. __ I am here for you. Have faith,
be - lieve in me. __ Have faith, be - lieve __ in me. __
I am here for you. Be - lieve!

VERSES

1. Je - sus, you're __ so good __ to us, __
2. You fill us with __ your love __ and light, __
3. We praise you, Je - sus, ev - 'ry day, __

1. ev - 'ry day __ so good to __ us. __
2. live in us __ as love and __ light. __
3. praise and thank __ you ev - 'ry __ day. __

Once there was a man who lived in a town called Capernaum. He had a son who was very, very sick. He was so sick that his father thought he was dying.

The father heard that Jesus was in the town of Cana, which was a long way from Capernaum. But the man believed that Jesus could make his son better, so he decided to walk all the way from Capernaum to Cana to find Jesus.

It was a long, long walk and the road was hilly and the man was very tired. At last he came to Cana and he found Jesus. He begged Jesus to hurry back to Capernaum with him to heal his son. He said, "Please, Jesus, come before my little boy dies. I know you can make him better." Jesus saw that the man loved his little boy very much and he wanted to help him. So Jesus said to the father, "Your little boy is better now. I have healed him. Go home and see." The little boy's father believed Jesus had healed his son, and he hurried all the way back to Capernaum. He was hurrying as fast as he could because he wanted to see his little boy.

While he was on his way, a servant from his house came running to find him and said, "Sir, your child is all right. He's not sick any more. He is better." The father was so happy. He asked, "When did my little boy get better?" The servant said, "It was yesterday about one o'clock in the afternoon." The little boy's father said, "That is the very same time that Jesus said to me, 'Your little boy is better.'" And he went home to see his son and tell the family what Jesus had done. After that, everyone in the man's family believed in Jesus.

Jesus, Help Us

Capo 1: **(G)**
Ab

(C/G)
Db/Ab

1. The wind was blow-ing and blow-ing and blow-ing, the
2. the wind is blow-ing and blow-ing and blow-ing, the

(G)
Ab

(A/G)
Bb/Ab

(Em)
Fm

1. light-'ning flash-ing and flash-ing. The waves were crash-ing and
2. light-'ning flash-ing and flash-ing. The waves are crash-ing and

(F#/A#)
G/B

(Em)
Fm

(F#m)
Gm

(B+)
C+

1. crash-ing and crash-ing, the wa-ter was splash-ing and splash-ing.
2. crash-ing and crash-ing, the wa-ter is splash-ing and splash-ing.

(Am6)
Bbm6

(Em/G)
Fm/Ab

(Am6)
Bbm6

1-2. Help us, Je-sus. Lord, we need _ you. We don't know what to

(B)
C

(F#7)
G7

(B)
C

1-2. do. Je-sus, help us. Lord, we need you, don't you see?

1
(Am) **(D7)**
Bbm Eb7

2
(Am) **(B7)**
Bbm C7

1-2. Don't you see that 2. see?_____ "Yes, I see."

(A7/E)
Bb7/F

(B/D#)
C/E

(A/C#)
Bb/D

3. Then Je - sus said to the

26

3. wind, "Stop blow-ing and blow-ing and blow-ing and light-'ning flash-ing and

3. flash-ing,   and waves stop crash-ing and crash-ing and crash-ing and

3. wa-ter STOP splash-ing and splash-ing." And all   at   once   at   the

3. voice   of   Je - sus   the   wind stopped   blow-ing,   the

3. light-'ning stopped flash-ing,   the waves stopped crash-ing and the

3. wa-ter stopped splash - ing. ___ And ev-'ry-thing was calm, there was

3. no   more storm.   Ev-'ry-thing was calm, there was no   more

3. storm.   Ev - 'ry-thing was calm, there was no   more   storm.

One day Jesus was sitting by the side of Lake Galilee with his friends. There were lots of other people there, too, who came to listen to Jesus. Jesus was teaching them about what heaven is like. The people always loved to hear Jesus speaking.

Later, when Jesus had finished and it was getting dark, he said to his friends, "Let's go over to the other side of the lake." So Jesus and his friends got into the boat and rowed out into the lake. Jesus was very tired because he had been teaching all day. Now in the back of the boat there was a place to lie down. So Jesus lay down, put his head on a pillow and went to sleep.

While he was sleeping, it began to rain. Then the wind started blowing and it rained very hard. The wind blew harder and harder, and the storm was very frightening. The wind was blowing so hard that waves of water were splashing right into the boat. Jesus' friends were so scared they didn't know what to do! They saw the water coming into the boat and they thought that the boat was going to sink. They went and shook Jesus and woke him up and cried out, "Jesus, help us! Look, our boat is sinking and we're going to drown!"

Jesus got up, looked at the wind and shouted, "Wind, stop blowing!" And he said to the water, "Water, be still!" And do you know what happened? At once the wind *did* stop blowing and the water did become very still.

Then Jesus said to his friends, "Why are you afraid? Believe in me. I will take care of you." His friends were amazed and said, "Who is this man? He can make the wind stop blowing and the water become still."

What Can I Give To God?

A long time ago, when Jesus lived in Nazareth, some people had a very bad disease called leprosy. Leprosy made sores on a person's body. The sores hurt a lot and were very ugly. No one wanted to be near a person with leprosy in case they got it too, because once someone caught leprosy, they could never be made well. Even doctors couldn't cure them. So the people with leprosy wrapped their sores in rags and lived in caves, away from everyone else.

Now one day a man who had leprosy saw Jesus walking with his disciples. He had heard about Jesus and all the wonderful things he had done for other people – how he had healed them and made them well. The man believed that Jesus could cure him, too. So he went to Jesus and begged him saying, "Lord, I know you can cure me if you want to." Jesus felt very sorry for the man with leprosy. And even though no one ever touched people with leprosy, Jesus put his hand out, touched the man and said, "Yes, I do want to cure you. Be healed." At once the man was healed. His sores were all gone and his leprosy was completely healed.

Jesus said to the man, "Go now to the priest and show him that you are cured. And remember, take a gift to God to say 'thank you' because you have been healed." The man was happy and ran off to show the priest that he was healed, and he brought his gift for God.

Wonderful Things

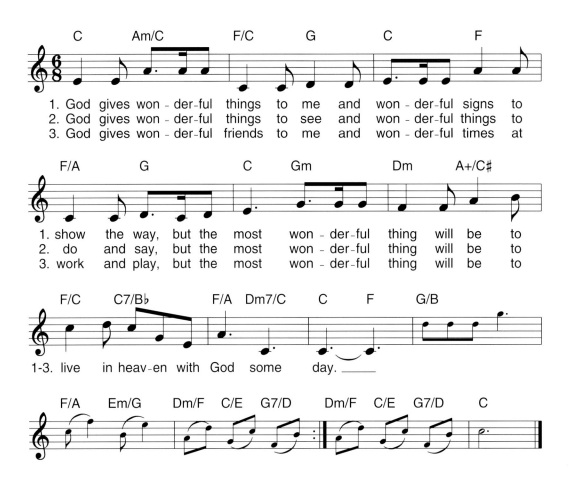

1. God gives won - der-ful things to me and won - der-ful signs to
2. God gives won - der-ful things to see and won - der-ful things to
3. God gives won - der-ful friends to me and won - der-ful times at

1. show the way, but the most won - der-ful thing will be to
2. do and say, but the most won - der-ful thing will be to
3. work and play, but the most won - der-ful thing will be to

1-3. live in heav-en with God some day. _____

Jesus wanted his friends to know how wonderful heaven is. So he told them this story to help them understand.

Once there was a man who bought and sold very special pearls. He traveled all over the world to find the best pearls so that he could sell them. On one of his trips he found a wonderful pearl. It was the most beautiful pearl he had ever seen in his life, and it cost a lot of money. The man said, "This is the most beautiful pearl I have ever seen! But I don't have enough money to buy it." So he thought for a moment, and then he said, "I know what I'll do. I'll sell everything I have so I can buy that beautiful pearl." And that's just what he did. The man sold everything he had and went and bought the beautiful pearl. Jesus said, "Heaven is like that pearl. It is worth everything we have."

The Lord's Prayer

*Our Fa - ther, who art in heav - en, hal - lowed be thy
Our Fa - ther in heav - en, hal - lowed be your

name; thy king - dom come; __ thy will be done on earth
name, your king - dom come, __ your will be done, on earth

as it is in heav - en. Give us this day our dai - ly bread; and for -
as in heav - en. Give us to - day our dai - ly bread. For -

give us our tres - pas - ses ___ as we for - give those _ who
give us our sins _____ as we for - give those _ who

tres - pass a - gainst _ us; ___ and lead us not ___ in - to temp -
sin a - gainst us. __ Save _ us from the time of

ta - tion, but de - liv - er us from e - vil.
tri - al and de - liv - er us from e - vil. For the

king - dom, the pow - er, and the glo - ry are yours, now and for

ev - er. A - men, a - men. ___

*for use in liturgy

Jesus loved to pray to God. Sometimes he went away by himself and prayed for a long time, even all night long. Jesus always prayed before he did miracles and before he taught his disciples.

His disciples wanted to learn to pray like him. So one day they said, "Jesus, teach us how to pray." Jesus said to them, "Pray like this:

Our Father in heaven,
hallowed be your name,
your kingdom come,
your will be done,
on earth as in heaven.
Give us today our daily bread.
Forgive us our sins
as we forgive those who sin against us.
Save us from the time of trial
and deliver us from evil."

And Jesus said to them, "Ask God for what you need, and God will answer your prayer."

Who Am I?

Jesus used to go everywhere teaching people about God. Lots of people came to hear Jesus, but some of them didn't know who he really was.

One day when Jesus was talking alone with his friends, he asked them, "What are other people saying about me? Who do they say I am?" His friends told him, "Some people think you are the prophet, Elijah. And some people think you are John the Baptist. Other people say you are Jeremiah, or some other prophet."

Then Jesus looked at them and asked them, "But you, who do you say I am?"

Peter said to Jesus, "You are Jesus, the Christ. You are the Son of God." Jesus said, "Peter, you are right. And you are blessed because God told you who I am."

Then Jesus said, "Peter, your name means 'rock.' And your faith is just like a rock. On this rock of faith, I will build my church. And my church will always be strong. Nothing will ever destroy it."

Jesus Wants To Help Us

1. We be-lieve Je-sus wants to help us. We be-lieve Je-sus wants to
2. When we pray, Je-sus wants to hear us. When we pray, Je-sus wants to
3. Ev -'ry day Je-sus is be-side us. Ev - 'ry day Je-sus is be-

1. help us. We be-lieve that Je - sus al-ways wants to help us.
2. hear us. We be-lieve that Je - sus al-ways wants to hear us.
3. side us. We be-lieve that Je - sus al-ways is be - side us.

One day Jesus met a man who had a crippled hand. He couldn't move it. He couldn't pick things up. He couldn't use it at all. Jesus felt sorry for the man and said, "I want to help you." The man said, "Jesus, I believe that you can help me." So Jesus said to the man, "Hold out your hand." The man held out his crippled hand just like Jesus had asked him. As he held out his hand, it was completely healed so that he could move it and use it just like his other hand.

When the people saw that Jesus had healed the man's hand, they said, "Let's bring all the people we know who are sick so that Jesus can heal them, too." Some people just wanted to touch Jesus. When they saw all the wonderful things Jesus did, they said, "Jesus, you are truly the Son of God."

I'll Find My Friend

Jesus wants us to know that God loves us very much. So one time he told this story.

Once there was a woman who had ten silver coins. They were very precious to her and she had kept these ten coins for a long time. One day when she was looking at her coins, she counted them and found there were only nine. One of the coins was missing. She had lost it. The woman looked everywhere for the lost coin. She said, "I must find my silver coin." She looked all over the house, but she couldn't find it. Then she got a broom and swept the floor, under the bed and everywhere. She looked and looked and looked. And at last she found her silver coin.

The woman was so happy that she ran to her friends and neighbors and said, "Look, I have found my precious coin that I lost. Come to my house and celebrate with me." So all of her friends came, and they had a big party because everyone was glad that the woman had found her lost coin.

After Jesus told this story, he said to his friends, "Do you know what? God is just like that woman in the story. When someone is lost, God looks and looks and looks. And when the lost person is found, God and all the angels are very, very happy."

The Pharisee And The Sinner

Once, Jesus said to his friends, "I want you to know that God is happy when we are honest and tell God we are sorry when we do something wrong." Then he told them this story.

One day two people went up to the temple to pray. One was a Pharisee and one was a sinner. The Pharisee was a leader in his religion. He always did what the law said was right. The sinner did things that were wrong. He had cheated some people out of their money and he didn't always tell the truth. The man who was a Pharisee thought he was very important and that God loved him more because he followed all the rules. He went to the front of the temple where everyone could see him and he prayed out loud. He said, "O God, I thank you that I am so good. You know that I am not a sinner. I don't steal, I don't lie, and I don't cheat like he does." And he pointed to the other man. Then he said, "I give money to the church. I do lots of good things."

But the sinner stayed in the back where no one could see him. He bowed his head and prayed very quietly. He said, "O God, please forgive me. I know that I do things that are wrong, but I want to change. I want to do good things. Please help me."

Jesus said to his friends, "I tell you that God did help him and did forgive that sinner. And that man went home happy."

You Give Us Life

Jesus and his friends used to go all over the countryside teaching everyone about God. One day they came to a town called Nain. When they got there, they saw a large crowd of people and one of the disciples said, "I wonder what is happening in this little town. Why are all these people so sad?" Then they saw that a young man had died and his friends were taking him to be buried. The mother of the young man was there. She was a widow because her husband had died, and the young man was her only son. She was crying so hard – no one knew what to say to help her. Many people were trying to comfort her.

When Jesus saw the mother so sad, he felt very sorry for her and said to her, "Don't cry. I will help you." Then he said to the people who were carrying the young man, "Stop!" Jesus went over and touched the dead man and said, "Young man, I tell you, get up!" And what do you think happened? Right away the dead man got up and began to talk.

All the people were amazed and could hardly believe what Jesus had done. Jesus took the young man over to his mother. She was so happy that her son was alive again. She said, "Thank you, Jesus, thank you for giving me back my son." The people who were with her said, "Jesus is a great man and he really cares about us." And they told everyone they met about what Jesus had done for the widow at Nain.

The Sower

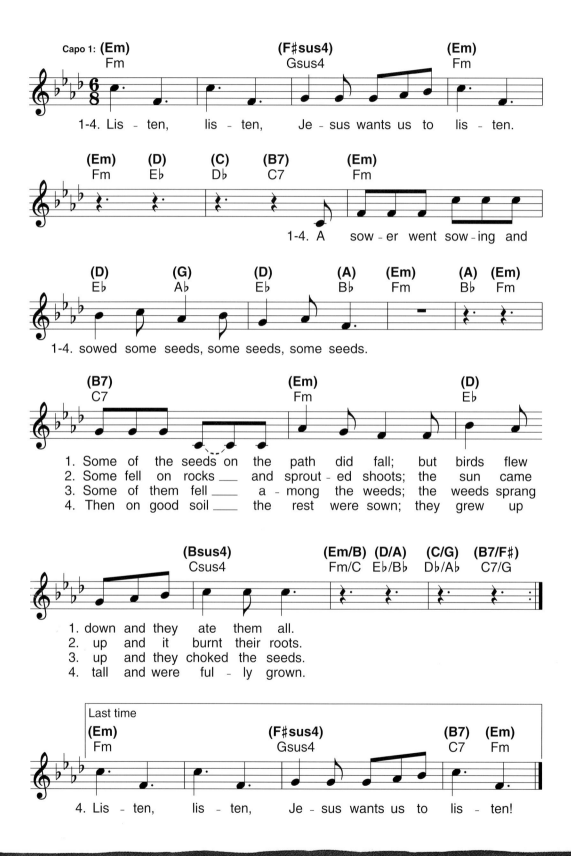

Lots of people used to come and hear Jesus tell them stories about how to be kind and fair to one another. Sometimes Jesus would go down to the beach and sit in a boat and talk to the people. They would come and sit on the sand and listen to everything Jesus told them. One day when there was a big crowd, Jesus told them this story.

Once there was a sower who went out to sow seeds in the ground. Some of the seeds fell on a path. They stayed on top of the ground, and the birds came and ate them all up.

The sower sowed some more seeds, but they fell on ground that had lots of rocks in it. The dirt wasn't very deep and there wasn't enough water. The seeds grew into plants quickly, but they weren't very strong. So in the afternoon, when the sun got very hot, they were all burned and dried up.

The sower planted some more seeds, and they fell into some bushes that had thorns. But the thorns were stronger than the plants and grew bigger and choked the plants so they couldn't grow.

Then the sower sowed some more seeds, and these seeds fell into the good ground. It had good deep dirt and lots of water. So, the plants grew and grew and became tall and strong.

Then Jesus said to the people, "The good ground is like people who hear what I am saying and believe it in their heart. They listen and do what I say, and my words grow strong in them."

God's Special Joy

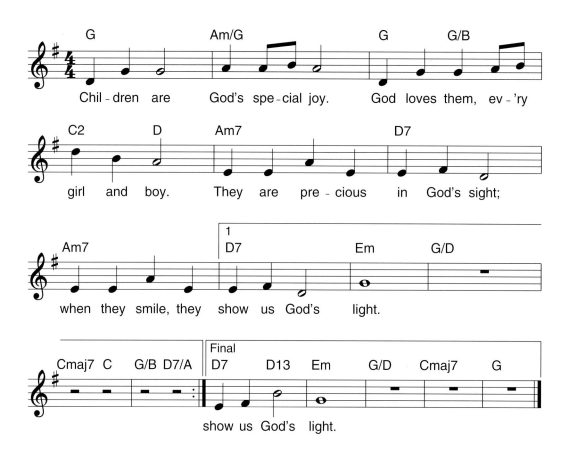

Chil – dren are God's spe – cial joy. God loves them, ev – 'ry
girl and boy. They are pre – cious in God's sight;
when they smile, they show us God's light.
show us God's light.

One day Jesus and his friends were walking in the country. Jesus was walking by himself ahead of the others. His friends began asking each other, "Which one of us is the most important? Who is the greatest?" Jesus stopped, turned around and asked them, "What are you talking about?" They said, "Jesus, we want to know who is the best, who is the greatest, which one of us is the most important?"

Just then, Jesus saw a little child and he said to her, "Please come over here with me." So the little girl went and stood right next to Jesus. Jesus put his arm around her and said to his friends, "If you want to see the kingdom of heaven, you have to be just like this little child. Children are honest and they don't think they are better than anyone else. And if you are honest, you will see the kingdom of heaven."

Then Jesus said, "If you are my true friends, you will help other people, and then you will be great in the kingdom of heaven."

Sing Hosanna

Every year many people went to the great city called Jerusalem to celebrate the special day called Passover. One year as they went on their way to Jerusalem, Jesus said to two of his friends, "Go into the next town and when you get there you will see a donkey tied to a post. Untie it and bring it to me. If anyone asks you, 'Why are you taking that donkey?' say to them, 'Jesus needs it, but he will bring it back.'"

So the two friends went into the town and they found the donkey, just as Jesus said they would. While they were untying it some of the people asked, 'Why are you taking that donkey?" His friends said, "Jesus needs it, but he will bring it back." So they let Jesus' friends take the donkey. They brought it to Jesus, put their coats on its back and put Jesus on the donkey so that he could ride into Jerusalem.

There were lots of people and they were excited to see Jesus, and they shouted, "Blessed is the Lord." Then someone in the crowd said, "Let's cut branches from the palm trees and put them on the road, like a carpet for Jesus, our king."

Everyone praised God for all the wonderful things Jesus had done. The children ran ahead of Jesus, waving palm branches and singing, "Hosanna! Hosanna in the highest. Hosanna! Hosanna to the king."

Love Each Other

Capo 3: (Em) / Gm — (Am7) / Cm7 — (B7) / D7

1. On the night Jesus died, he __ said ____ to his friends,
2. Then he went to his friends and be-gan to wash their feet.
3. "You __ don't un-der-stand, but __ la - ter you will."
4. "I have done this to show you __ what ____ you must do."
5. To - day we will do what __ Je - sus has said:

(Em) / Gm — (Am) / Cm — (D7) / F7 — (G) / Bb

1-5. "Help each oth - er. _____ Love each oth - er, _____ as

(C) / Eb — (G/B) / Bb/D — (Am7) / Cm7 — (B7) / D7 — (Em) / Gm — (Am7) / Cm7

1-5. I have loved you, as I have loved you."

(Em) / Gm — (F#) / A — (Bsus4) / Dsus4 — (B7) / D7 — 1-4 (Em) / Gm — Final (Em) / Gm

On the night before Jesus died, he was having supper with some of his friends. It was a very special supper called Passover. Everyone was talking and eating and having a good time.

While they were eating, Jesus did something that his friends didn't understand at all. He got up from the table and took off his robe. He tied a towel around his waist and poured water into a bowl. Then he went to each of his friends, knelt down in front of them and began to wash their feet. Nobody knew why he was doing that, so they just watched. But when he came to Peter and was about to wash his feet, Peter said, "Lord, you're not going to wash my feet, are you?" Jesus said, "Yes, Peter, I am." Peter said, "But you are the Lord. You shouldn't wash my feet." Jesus said, "Peter, you don't understand this now, but you will understand later." And Jesus washed Peter's feet.

After Jesus had washed the feet of all his friends, he put his robe back on, sat down at the table again and asked them, "Do you know why I washed your feet?" They didn't know, so they didn't say anything. Jesus said, "I washed your feet because I want to show you that we should help each other. If you love each other and help each other, everyone will see that you are my friends. So love each other, just as I love you."

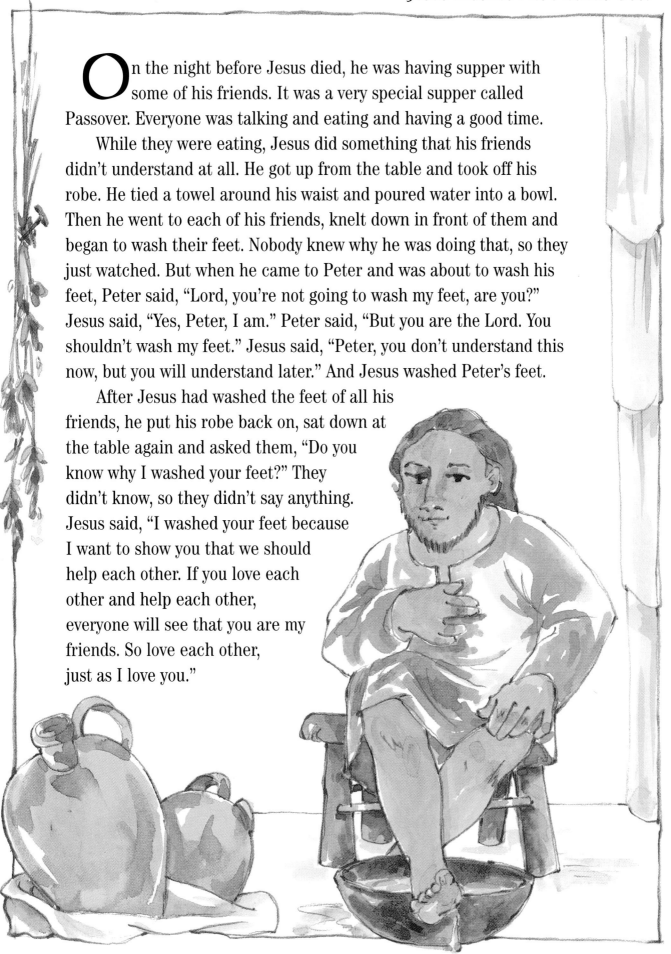

I Am Your Friend

REFRAIN

Capo 1: **(D7)** **(G)** **(C/G)** **(G/B)**
Eb7   Ab   Db/Ab   Ab/C

I am your friend, _____ al – ways here be –

(Em) **(C)** **(G/B)** **(Am7)** **(G)**
Fm   Db   Ab/C   Bbm7   Ab

side you, __ to watch and be with you in all that you do. __

(C) **(D7)** **(G)**
Db   Eb7   Ab   *Fine*

____ I am your friend, I am your friend.

VERSES

(Asus4) **(Am)** **(Gsus4)** **(G)**
Bbsus4   Bbm   Absus4   Ab

1. We will fol – low Je – sus' way, to his cross, with him we
2. Je – sus helps us ev – 'ry day in the fears that come our

(Am7) **(C/G)** **(D7)**
Bbm7   Db/Ab   Eb7   *D.C.*

1. stay, in our hearts to him _____ we say:
2. way, in our hearts we hear _____ him say:

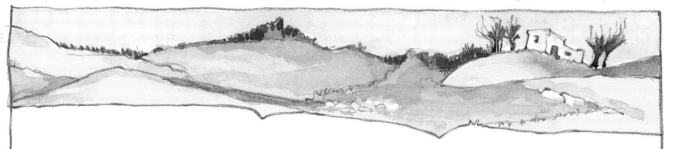

Do you remember that the night before Jesus died, he had a special supper with his friends? When the supper was over, they sang a blessing song and then they all went out to a garden called Gethsemane.

Jesus said to his friends, "I am frightened about what is going to happen to me. Wait here, while I go over there to pray. Stay awake and pray with me." So Jesus went a little further into the garden and he knelt down and said, "O God, I know that you love me and that you can do anything. Take this fear away from me. I don't want to suffer. But I will do whatever you want me to do." Jesus was shaking with fear. Then an angel from heaven came to Jesus and said, "Be strong. Even if you suffer, God is with you."

When Jesus went back to his friends, they weren't praying. They were all asleep. Jesus said to them, "Wake up! Why are you sleeping? Stay awake and pray that you will be strong no matter what happens."

Now Judas was a friend of Jesus, but he turned against him. He went to the leaders who wanted to kill Jesus and said, "I know where Jesus is. If you pay me, I will take you to him." So they paid him thirty pieces of silver and he took them to the garden where Jesus was. Judas said, "There he is! That's Jesus." The people grabbed Jesus and took him to the leader whose name was Pilate. All the people shouted, "Kill him, kill him!" Pilate asked, "Why? What has Jesus done wrong?" They said, "He says he is the Son of God, and he isn't. He is pretending to be God. He should die."

So Pilate let them take Jesus away to kill him. The soldiers made Jesus carry a big cross. A lot of people followed him and when they got to the top of the hill, the soldiers nailed Jesus to the cross.

After Jesus died, his friends took him off the cross and buried him in a tomb.

I Am Here With You

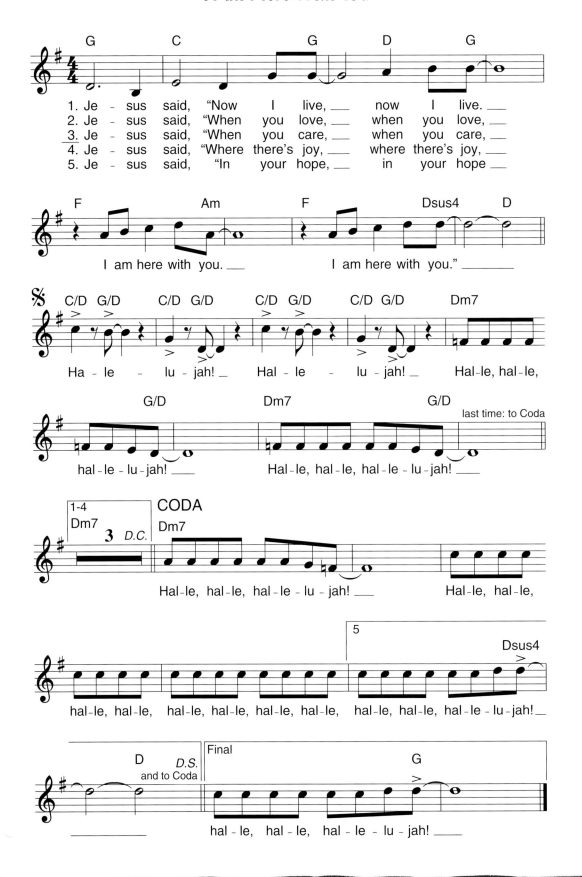

It was very early on Sunday morning, two days after Jesus was buried. Everything was quiet and dark. Before the sun came up, Mary Magdalen went to the tomb where Jesus was buried to put special oils on his body. Even though Mary Magdalen was a sinner, Jesus had been very kind to her. She loved him very much. Mary missed Jesus and she stood by the tomb crying.

When she bent down and looked into the tomb, she couldn't see Jesus. He was not there. Two angels were sitting where the body of Jesus had been. One of the angels said to Mary, "Why are you crying?" She said, "Where is Jesus? Someone has taken him away and I don't know where he is." The angel said, "Jesus is not here because he is alive."

Suddenly Mary Magdalen heard someone call her name, "Mary!" She turned around and saw a man, and he said again, "Mary!" It was Jesus calling her name! Mary said, "Jesus, it's really you! You are alive!" She ran to Jesus and hugged him. Jesus said, "Go and tell my friends I am alive and I will see them in Galilee."

So Mary ran back to the disciples and said, "I have seen the Lord. He is alive! Go to Galilee and you will see him!"

Together We'll Share

What does the world need? ___ What does the world need? _

_ The world needs peace, the world needs peace.

*[hope, food, love, joy]   [hope, food, love, joy]

REFRAIN

You bring some, and I'll bring some, and to-geth-er we'll

share. You bring some, and I'll bring some, and to-

geth-er we'll share with the world.

*Ask the children for suggestions.

58

Do you remember the story of how Jesus rose from the dead? After Jesus died, his friends thought they would never see him again. But God raised Jesus from the dead. After he rose from the dead, Jesus went to see his friends at Lake Galilee. This is how it happened.

One day Peter was with his friends, Thomas, Nathaniel, James and John. They were sad because Jesus had died. They didn't know that Jesus was alive again. Peter said to his friends, "I am going fishing." They said, "We'll go with you, Peter." So they all got into a boat and rowed out on the lake. They fished and fished for a long time. They fished all night long. But they didn't catch any fish.

Very early the next morning, when the sun was just rising, they saw Jesus standing on the beach, but they didn't know it was Jesus. Jesus saw his friends in the boat and called out to them, "Did you catch any fish?" They said, "No, we didn't." So Jesus said to them, "Try again and this time you will catch some." So they put their nets back into the water. And do you know what? They caught lots and lots of fish. They caught so many fish that they couldn't pull the net out of the water!

When they rowed the boat closer to the beach, they saw Jesus standing by a little fire. He was cooking some bread. Peter said, "Look, it's Jesus!" Peter was so excited that he jumped into the water and swam to the shore. He ran up to Jesus and said, "Jesus, you are alive!" His friends dragged the boat with the net full of fish onto the beach. Jesus said to Peter, "Bring some of the fish you have caught and let's cook them." So Peter brought some fish and put them with the bread on the fire to cook.

Then Jesus said, "Come and have breakfast." And he gave them all some bread and fish. The disciples were very happy to see Jesus alive again and to share a meal with him.

Come, Feed My Sheep

After Jesus and his friends had eaten breakfast on the beach, Jesus and Peter went for a little walk. While they were walking, Jesus asked Peter, "Peter, do you love me?" Peter said, "Yes, Lord, I do love you." Jesus said to Peter, "I want you to feed my sheep." And they walked on.

Then Jesus asked Peter again, "Peter, do you really love me?" Peter said, "Yes, Jesus, I really do love you." Jesus said again, "Peter, feed my sheep." And they walked on.

When Jesus asked Peter the third time, "Peter, do you love me more than anyone?" Peter said, "Jesus, you know everything. You know how much I love you." Jesus said, "Feed my sheep." Jesus was really asking Peter to take care of his people.

Then Jesus said to Peter, "Follow me." And they walked on together.

Christopher Walker, internationally-known lecturer, composer and conductor, was born and educated in England, attending Bristol University where he earned his degree. He served as Director of Music at Clifton Cathedral in Bristol and Director of Music for the Clifton Diocese.

Christopher is presently residing in Los Angeles where he is a music lecturer at Mount St. Mary's College and also the musician for the Family Mass at St. Paul the Apostle Church. From there, he travels to many countries giving workshops for church musicians and teachers, and giving retreats for parishes.

His music is sung all over the world in many languages. His compositions have been published in the St. Thomas More Group collections: *Sing Of The Lord's Goodness; We Are Your People; Lead Me, O Lord; Come To Set Us Free;* and *Holy Is God.* His own published works are *Music For Children's Liturgy Of The Word, Out Of Darkness, Calling The Children, Christ Is Here* and *The Celtic Mass.*

Paule Freeburg, DC, is Religion Consultant for the Diocese of San Jose, CA. With a degree in Speech and Hearing and a graduate degree in Theology, she has an extensive background working in Religious Education with both children and adults. Paule has taught elementary and high school; she has served as Director of Religious Education and has directed Sacramental programs for children; she has directed parish RCIA programs and presented RCIA institutes in the USA and England.

Paule currently works in Development and Public Relations at a school for economically disadvantaged children. She presents workshops around the USA on the Spirituality of Children and Celebrating the Word with Children. She is primary author of the biblical material for *Sunday,* a Liturgy of the Word for Children series, and is co-author of *A Child Shall Lead them* (Treehaus Communications, Inc.).

Jean Germano is a graduate of FIT in New York City. She worked as an illustrator in New York before relocating to Rome, Italy. There she worked for the North American College as well as the Bishop's Office for Visitors. After spending fifteen years in Rome, Jean moved with her husband and two children to Portland, Oregon. She began doing freelance art for Oregon Catholic Press and in 1986 became their Art Director.

Jean dedicates the art in this book to Michael, Molly, Sarah and Madeline.

Gospel References